MARQUEE SERIES

P9-DTT-503

Microsoft®
PowerPoint®
2016

Workbook

Nita Rutkosky
Pierce College Puyallup
Puyallup, Washington

Audrey Roggenkamp
Pierce College Puyallup
Puyallup, Washington

Ian Rutkosky
Pierce College Puyallup
Puyallup, Washington

PARADIGM
EDUCATION SOLUTIONS

St. Paul

Senior Vice President	Linda Hein
Editor in Chief	Christine Hurney
Director of Production	Timothy W. Larson
Production Editors	Rachel Kats, Jen Weaverling
Cover and Text Designer	Valerie King
Copy Editor	Sarah Kearin
Senior Design and Production Specialist	Jaana Bykonich
Assistant Developmental Editors	Mamie Clark, Katie Werdick
Testers	Desiree Carvel; Ann E. Mills, Ivy Tech Community College of Indiana, Indianapolis, IN
Instructional Support Writer	Brienna McWade
Indexer	Terry Casey
Vice President Information Technology	Chuck Bratton
Digital Projects Manager	Tom Modl
Vice President Sales and Marketing	Scott Burns
Director of Marketing	Lara Weber McLellan

Care has been taken to verify the accuracy of information presented in this book. However, the authors, editors, and publisher cannot accept responsibility for Web, email, newsgroup, or chat room subject matter or content, or for consequences from application of the information in this book, and make no warranty, expressed or implied, with respect to its content.

Trademarks: Microsoft is a trademark or registered trademark of Microsoft Corporation in the United States and/or other countries. Some of the product names and company names included in this book have been used for identification purposes only and may be trademarks or registered trade names of their respective manufacturers and sellers. The authors, editors, and publisher disclaim any affiliation, association, or connection with, or sponsorship or endorsement by, such owners.

Cover Photo Credits: © whitehoune/Shutterstock.com; © Bohbeh/Shutterstock.com.

We have made every effort to trace the ownership of all copyrighted material and to secure permission from copyright holders. In the event of any question arising as to the use of any material, we will be pleased to make the necessary corrections in future printings. Thanks are due to the aforementioned authors, publishers, and agents for permission to use the materials indicated.

ISBN: 978-0-76387-146-8 (print)
ISBN: 978-0-76386-724-9 (digital)

© 2017 by Paradigm Publishing, Inc.
875 Montreal Way
St. Paul, MN 55102
Email: educate@emcp.com
Website: ParadigmCollege.com

Printed in the United States of America

24 23 22 21 20 19 18 17   5 6 7 8 9 10 11 12

Microsoft®

PowerPoint®

Study Tools

Study tools include a presentation and In Brief step lists. Use these resources to help you further develop and review skills learned in this section.

Knowledge Check

SNAP Check your understanding by identifying application tools used in this section. If you are a SNAP user, launch the Knowledge Check from your Assignments page.

Recheck

SNAP Check your understanding by taking this quiz. If you are a SNAP user, launch the Recheck from your Assignments page.

Skills Exercise

SNAP Additional activities are available to SNAP users. If you are a SNAP user, access these activities from your Assignments page.

Skills Review

 **Review 1   Creating a Presentation for Marquee Productions**

1. With a blank presentation open in PowerPoint, click the Design tab and then click the *Facet* option in the Themes group.
2. Type the title and subtitle for Slide 1 as shown in Figure WB-1.1.
3. Click the Home tab and then click the New Slide button in the Slides group.
4. Type the text shown for Slide 2 in Figure WB-1.1.
5. Continue creating the slides for the presentation as shown in Figure WB-1.1.
6. Insert a new Slide 3 between the current Slides 2 and 3 with the text shown in Figure WB-1.2.
7. Display Slide 2 in the slide pane and then change the slide layout to *Title Slide*.
8. Click in the text *Current Status* to select the placeholder and then move the placeholder up approximately one inch.
9. Click in the text *Overview of project* to select the placeholder and then move the placeholder up approximately one-half inch.
10. Change to Slide Sorter view and then move Slide 3 (*Resources*) immediately after Slide 1 (*Marquee Productions*).
11. Change to Normal view, click the Transitions tab, click the More Transitions button in the gallery in the Transition to This Slide group, and then click the *Orbit* option in the *Dynamic Content* section.

12. Click the *Sound* option box arrow and then click *Drum Roll* at the drop-down list.
13. Click the *Duration* measurement box down arrow until *00.75* displays in the measurement box.
14. Apply the transition, sound, and duration to all slides in the presentation.
15. Save the presentation with the name **1-MPTeamMtg**.
16. Run the slide show beginning with Slide 1.
17. View the presentation as an outline in the Print backstage area.
18. Print the presentation with all five slides displayed horizontally on one page.
19. Save and then close **1-MPTeamMtg.pptx**.

Figure WB-1.1 Review 1

Slide 1	Title	Marquee Productions
	Subtitle	Location Team Meeting
Slide 2	Title	Current Status
	Bullets	• Overview of project
		• Tasks on schedule
		• Tasks behind schedule
Slide 3	Title	Filming Sites
	Bullets	• Gardiner Expressway
		• Kings Mill Park
		• Island Airport
		• Royal Ontario Museum
		• Black Creek Pioneer Village
		• Additional sites
Slide 4	Title	Key Issues
	Bullets	• Equipment rental
		• Budget overruns
		• Transportation concerns
		• Location agreements

Figure WB-1.2 Review 1

Slide 3	Title	Resources
	Bullets	• Location contacts
		• Movie extras
		• Catering company
		• Lodging
		• Transportation rentals

Skills Assessment

Assessment 1   Preparing a Presentation for Worldwide Enterprises

1. Prepare a presentation for Worldwide Enterprises with the information shown in Figure WB-1.3 below. (You determine the design theme.)
2. Add a transition, sound, and transition duration time of your choosing to all slides in the presentation.
3. Run the slide show.
4. Print the presentation with all five slides displayed horizontally on one page.
5. Save the presentation with the name **1-WEExecMtg**.
6. Close **1-WEExecMtg.pptx**.

Figure WB-1.3 Assessment 1

Slide 1	Title	Worldwide Enterprises
	Subtitle	Executive Meeting
Slide 2	Title	Accounting Policies
	Bullets	• Cash equivalents
		• Short-term investments
		• Inventory valuation
		• Property and equipment
		• Foreign currency translation
Slide 3	Title	Financial Instruments
	Bullets	• Investments
		• Derivative instruments
		• Credit risks
		• Fair value of instruments
Slide 4	Title	Inventories
	Bullets	• Products
		• Raw material
		• Equipment
		• Buildings
Slide 5	Title	Employee Plans
	Bullets	• Stock options
		• Bonus plan
		• Savings and retirement plan
		• Defined benefits plan
		• Foreign subsidiaries

Assessment 2   Preparing a Presentation for The Waterfront Bistro

1. Prepare a presentation for The Waterfront Bistro with the information shown in Figure WB-1.4 below. (You determine the design theme.)
2. Add a transition, sound, and transition duration time of your choosing to all slides in the presentation.
3. Run the slide show.
4. Print the presentation with all five slides displayed horizontally on one page.
5. Save the presentation with the name **1-WBServices**.
6. Close **1-WBServices.pptx**.

Figure WB-1.4 Assessment 2

Slide 1	Title	The Waterfront Bistro
	Subtitle	3104 Rivermist Drive
		Buffalo, NY 14280
		(716) 555-3166
Slide 2	Title	Accommodations
	Bullets	• Dining area
		• Salon
		• Two banquet rooms
		• Wine cellar
Slide 3	Title	Menus
	Bullets	• Lunch
		• Dinner
		• Wines
		• Desserts
Slide 4	Title	Catering Services
	Bullets	• Lunch
		– Continental
		– Deli
		– Hot
		• Dinner
		– Vegetarian
		– Meat
		– Seafood
Slide 5	Title	Resource
	Subtitle	Dana Hirsch, Manager

Data File

Assessment 3   Finding Information on Setting Slide Show Timings

1. Open **MPProj.pptx** and then save the presentation with the name **1-MPProj**.
2. Use the Tell Me feature or experiment with the options on the Transitions tab to learn how to set slide show timings manually.
3. Set up the presentation so that, when running the slide show, each slide advances automatically after three seconds.
4. Run the slide show.
5. Save and then close **1-MPProj.pptx**.

Assessment 4 Preparing a Presentation on Cancun, Mexico

1. You are interested in planning a vacation to Cancun, Mexico. Connect to the Internet and search for information on Cancun. Locate information on lodging (hotels), restaurants, activities, and transportation.
2. Using PowerPoint, create a presentation about Cancun that contains the following:
   • Title slide with the title *Vacationing in Cancun* and your name as the subtitle
   • Slide containing the names of at least three major airlines that travel to Cancun
   • Slide containing the names of at least four hotels or resorts in Cancun
   • Slide containing the names of at least four restaurants in Cancun
   • Slide containing at least four activities in Cancun
3. Run the slide show.
4. Print all of the slides on one page.
5. Save the presentation with the name **1-Cancun**.
6. Close **1-Cancun.pptx**.

Marquee Challenge

FIRST CHOICE TRAVEL

Challenge 1   Preparing a Presentation on Toronto, Ontario, Canada

1. Create the presentation shown in Figure WB-1.5 on the next page. Apply the Basis design theme and the orange and white color variant. Apply appropriate slide layouts and size and move placeholders so your slides display as shown in the figure. (You will need to increase the size of the subtitle placeholder in Slide 6.)
2. Apply a transition, sound, and transition duration time of your choosing to each slide in the presentation.
3. Save the completed presentation with the name **1-FCTToronto**.
4. Print the presentation as a handout with all six slides displayed horizontally on one page.
5. Close the presentation.

Performance Threads

Data File

Challenge 2   Preparing a Presentation for Performance Threads

1. Open **PTCostumeMtg.pptx** and then save the presentation with the name **1-PTCostumeMtg**.
2. Apply the Organic design theme, add and rearrange slides, change slide layouts, and move a placeholder so the presentation displays as shown in Figure WB-1.6.
3. Apply a transition, sound, and transition duration time of your choosing to each slide in the presentation.
4. Save and then print the presentation as a handout with all six slides displayed horizontally on one page.
5. Close the presentation.

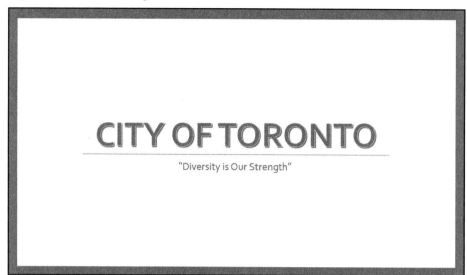

CITY OF TORONTO

"Diversity is Our Strength"

Museums and Galleries

- Royal Ontario Museum
- Art Gallery of Ontario
- Hockey Hall of Fame and Museum
- Ontario Science Centre
- Bata Shoe Museum

Theatres

- Toronto Centre for the Arts
- Betty Oliphant Theatre
- Massey Hall
- Premiere Dance Theatre
- Roy Thomson Hall
- Royal Alexandra
- Princess of Wales Theatre

continues

Sports Teams

- Baseball: Toronto Blue Jays
- Hockey: Toronto Maple Leafs
- Basketball: Toronto Raptors
- Football: Toronto Argonauts
- Soccer: Toronto FC

Tours

- Toronto Grand City Tour
- Harbour Cruise
- Toronto Dinner Cruise
- Medieval Times Dinner Show
- Vertical Obsession Helicopter Tour
- Niagara Falls Tour

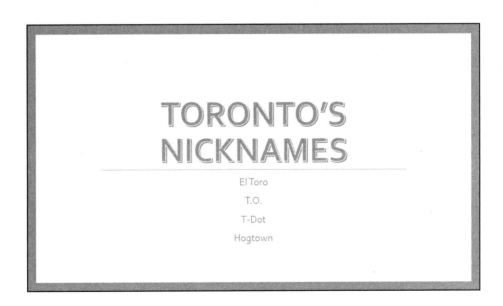

TORONTO'S NICKNAMES

El Toro

T.O.

T-Dot

Hogtown

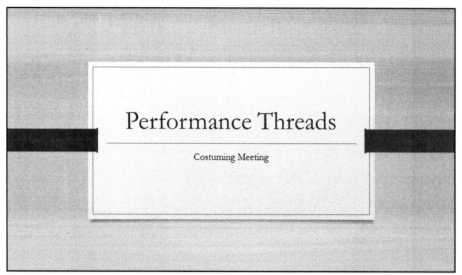

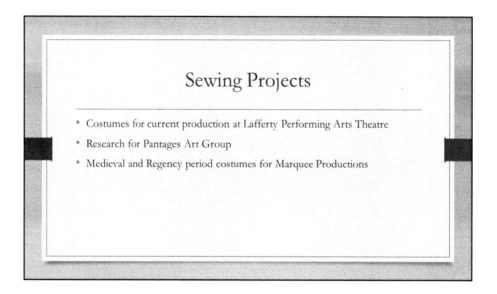

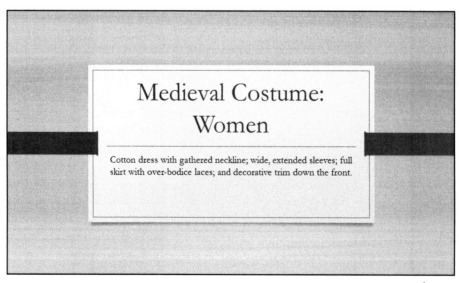

continues

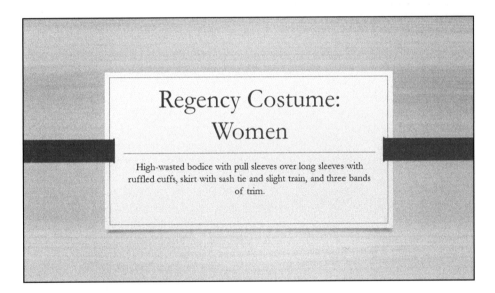

Study Tools

Study tools include a presentation and In Brief step lists. Use these resources to help you further develop and review skills learned in this section.

Knowledge Check

SNAP Check your understanding by identifying application tools used in this section. If you are a SNAP user, launch the Knowledge Check from your Assignments page.

Recheck

SNAP Check your understanding by taking this quiz. If you are a SNAP user, launch the Recheck from your Assignments page.

Skills Exercise

SNAP Additional activities are available to SNAP users. If you are a SNAP user, access these activities from your Assignments page.

Skills Review

Review 1 Editing and Formatting a Presentation for Marquee Productions

1. Open **MPMeeting.pptx** and then save it with the name **2-MPMeeting**.
2. Apply the Ion Boardroom design theme to the slides in the presentation, change the theme colors to Slipstream, and change the theme fonts to Arial Black - Arial.
3. Delete Slide 5 (contains the title *Financial*) in the slide thumbnails pane.
4. Change to Slide Sorter view and move Slide 7 (*Expenses*) immediately after Slide 3 (*Review of Goals*).
5. Move Slide 6 (*Future Goals*) immediately after the new Slide 7 (*Technology*).
6. Change to Normal view and then make Slide 4 (*Expenses*) the active slide.
7. Decrease the indent of *Payroll* so it displays aligned at the left with *Administration*.
8. Decrease the indent of *Benefits* so it displays aligned at the left with *Payroll* and *Administration*.
9. Make Slide 6 (*Technology*) active and then increase the indent of *Hardware* to the next level, the indent of *Software* to the next level, and the indent of *Technical Support* to the next level.
10. Make Slide 7 (*Future Goals*) active, select the name *Chris Greenbaum*, and then click the Copy button. (Make sure you select only the name and not the space following the name.)
11. Make Slide 3 (*Review of Goals*) active.

12. Move the insertion point immediately to the right of *Overview of Goals*, press the Enter key, press the Tab key, and then click the Paste button. (Clicking the Paste button inserts the name *Chris Greenbaum*. If an extra bullet displays below *Chris Greenbaum*, press the Backspace key two times.)

13. Move the insertion point immediately to the right of *Completed Goals*, press the Enter key, press the Tab key, and then click the Paste button. (Make sure an extra bullet does not display below *Chris Greenbaum*.)

14. Make Slide 7 (*Future Goals*) active, select the name *Shannon Grey* (do not include the space after the name), and then click the Copy button.

15. Make Slide 3 (*Review of Goals*) active and then paste the name *Shannon Grey* below *Goals Remaining* at the same tab location as *Chris Greenbaum*. (Make sure an extra bullet does not display below *Shannon Grey*.)

16. Paste the name *Shannon Grey* below *Analysis/Discussion* at the same tab location as *Chris Greenbaum*. (Make sure an extra bullet does not display below *Shannon Grey*.)

17. Make Slide 1 active, select the text *Marquee Productions*, change the font to Candara, change the font size to 60 points, and then apply bold formatting.

18. Select the text *ANNUAL MEETING*, change the font to Candara, change the font size to 36 points, and then apply bold formatting.

19. Make Slide 2 (*Agenda*) active, select the title *Agenda*, change the font to Candara, change the font size to 48 points, and then apply bold formatting.

20. Using Format Painter, apply the same formatting to the title in each of the remaining slides.

21. Make Slide 6 (*Technology*) active, select all of the bulleted text, and then change the line spacing to 1.5 lines.

22. Make Slide 8 (*Proposals*) active, select all of the bulleted text, and then change the spacing before paragraphs to 24 points.

23. Make Slide 2 (*Agenda*) active and then insert the image shown in Figure WB-2.1 with the following specifications:
    - Use the Pictures button on the Insert tab to insert the **Bullseye.png** image.
    - Apply the Blue, Accent color 1 Light color to the image (second column, third row in the *Recolor* section).
    - Change the height of the image to 4 inches.
    - Position the image as shown in the figure.

24. Make Slide 4 (*Expenses*) active and then insert the **DollarSymbol.png** image. Apply the Blue, Accent color 1 Light color to the image and change the height of the image to 3.3 inches. Position the image as shown in Figure WB-2.2.

25. Apply a transition, sound, and transition duration time to all slides in the presentation.

26. Run the slide show.

27. Print the presentation as handouts with four slides displayed horizontally per page.

28. Save and then close **2-MPMeeting.pptx**.

Figure WB-2.1 Review 1, Slide 2

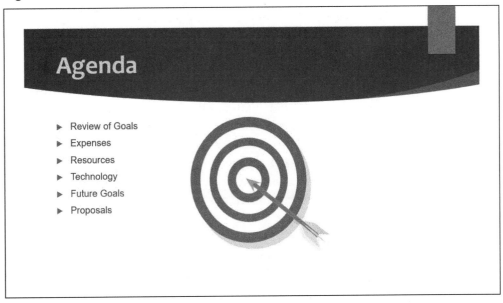

Figure WB-2.2 Review 1, Slide 4

Performance Threads

Data Files

Review 2   Formatting a Presentation for Performance Threads

1. Open **PTPres.pptx** and then save it with the name **2-PTPres**.
2. Change the slide size to Standard (4:3) and ensure the fit.
3. Change the design theme to Organic and the theme colors to Red.
4. With Slide 1 active, insert the **PTLogo.jpg** file. (Use the Pictures button in the Images group on the Insert tab.) Change the height of the logo to 2 inches and then position the logo in the middle of the slide.
5. Make the background of the logo transparent by clicking the Color button on the Picture Tools Format tab, clicking the *Set Transparent Color* option at the drop-down gallery, and then clicking anywhere in the white background of the logo.

6. Make Slide 3 active, select the bulleted text, and then change the line spacing to 1.5 lines.

7. Make Slide 4 active, select the bulleted text, and then change the spacing after paragraphs to 18 points.

8. Make Slide 2 active and then insert the SmartArt organizational chart shown in Figure WB-2.3 on the next page with the following specifications:
   - Click the *Hierarchy* option in the left panel of the Choose a SmartArt Graphic dialog box and then double-click the *Organization Chart* option.
   - Delete and add boxes so your organization chart has the same boxes as the one in Figure WB-2.3. ***Hint: Delete the single box in the middle row, delete one of the boxes in the bottom row, and then use the Add Shape button arrow and click Add Shape Below** to add the boxes in the bottom row.*
   - Type the text in the boxes. (Press Shift + Enter after entering the names.)
   - Apply the Colorful - Accent Colors color to the organizational chart (first option in the *Colorful* section).
   - Apply the Cartoon SmartArt style to the organizational chart (third column, first row in the *3-D* section).
   - Apply the Fill - Black, Text 1, Shadow WordArt style to the text in the shapes (first column, first row).

9. Make Slide 3 active and then insert the image shown in Figure WB-2.4 on the next page with the following specifications:
   - Use the Pictures button on the Insert tab to insert the **Medical.png** image.
   - Change the height of the image to 2.9 inches.
   - Change the color of the image to Dark Red, Accent color 1 Light (second column, third row in the *Recolor* section).
   - Apply the Brightness: 0% (Normal) Contrast: +40% brightness and contrast (third column, fifth row).
   - Position the image as shown in Figure WB-2.4.

10. Make Slide 5 active and then insert the SmartArt graphic shown in Figure WB-2.5 on the next page with the following specifications:
    - Click the *Process* option in the left panel at the Choose a SmartArt Graphic dialog box and then double-click *Alternating Flow*.
    - Apply the Colorful - Accent Colors color to the graphic (first option in the *Colorful* section).
    - Apply the Cartoon SmartArt style to the graphic (third column, first row in the *3-D* section).
    - Type the text in the boxes as shown in Figure WB-2.5.

11. Make Slide 2 active, click the SmartArt organizational chart, and then animate the organizational chart using options on the Animations tab. (You determine the type of animation.)

12. Make Slide 5 active, click the SmartArt graphic, and then animate the graphic using options on the Animations tab. (You determine the type of animation.)

13. Make Slide 3 active, click the bulleted text, and then apply the Split animation.

14. Make Slide 4 active, click the bulleted text, and then apply the Split animation.

15. Run the slide show.

16. Print the presentation as handouts with all five slides displayed horizontally on one page.

17. Save and then close **2-PTPres.pptx**.

Figure WB-2.3 Review 2, Slide 2

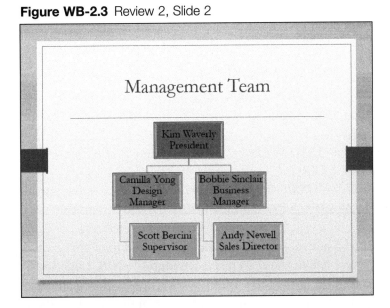

Figure WB-2.4 Review 2, Slide 3

Figure WB-2.5 Review 2, Slide 5

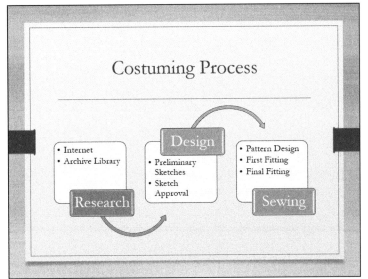

Skills Assessment

NIAGARA PENINSULA COLLEGE

Assessment 1 Formatting a Presentation for Niagara Peninsula College, Theatre Arts Division

Data Files

1. Open **NPCTheatreArts.pptx** and then save it with the name **2-NPCTheatreArts**.
2. Move Slide 7 (*ASSOCIATE DEGREES*) immediately after Slide 2 (*MISSION STATEMENT*).
3. Move Slide 6 (*SEMESTER COSTS*) immediately after the new Slide 7 (*FALL SEMESTER CLASSES*).
4. Make Slide 2 (*MISSION STATEMENT*) active, click in the paragraph below the title *MISSION STATEMENT*, and then justify the text alignment.
5. Change the line spacing to 1.5 lines for the bulleted text in Slides 5 and 7.
6. Make Slide 5 active, select the bulleted text, and then apply italic formatting.
7. Make Slide 1 active and then insert the logo file **NPCLogo.jpg** into the slide. Increase the size of the logo, set the background color as transparent, and then position the logo at the left side of the slide in the gray portion. ***Hint: Use the Color button in the Adjust group on the Picture Tools Format tab to set the background color as transparent.***
8. Make Slide 3 active and then insert a Radial Cycle SmartArt graphic (located in the *Cycle* category in the Choose a SmartArt Graphic dialog box) in the slide. Insert the text *Theatre Arts Division* in the middle circle and then insert the following text in the remaining four circles: *Production*, *Acting*, *Set Design*, and *Interactive Media*. Apply a color and SmartArt style of your choosing to the graphic. Apply any other formatting to enhance the appearance of the graphic. Position the graphic attractively on the slide.
9. Make Slide 4 active and then insert the Organization Chart SmartArt graphic (located in the *Hierarchy* category in the Choose a SmartArt Graphic dialog box) in the slide with the boxes and text shown in Figure WB-2.6. ***Hint: To add the extra box along the bottom, click the left box at the bottom, click the Add Shape button arrow, and then click*** **Add Shape Before.** Apply a color and SmartArt style of your choosing to the organizational chart. Apply any other formatting you desire to enhance the appearance of the organizational chart. Position the chart attractively on the slide.
10. Make Slide 7 active and then insert the **Money.png** image in the slide. Size, position, and recolor the image so it enhances the slide.
11. Make Slide 3 active and then apply an animation of your choosing to the SmartArt graphic.
12. Make Slide 4 active and then apply an animation of your choosing to the organizational chart.
13. Apply a transition, sound, and transition duration time of your choosing to all slides in the presentation.
14. Run the slide show.
15. Print the presentation as handouts with four slides displayed horizontally per page.
16. Save and then close **2-NPCTheatreArts.pptx**.

Figure WB-2.6 Assessment 1, SmartArt Organizational Chart

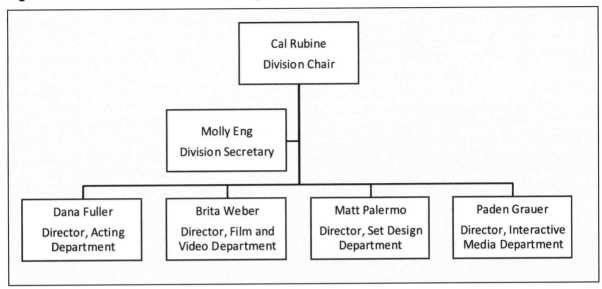

 Assessment 2 Formatting a Presentation for First Choice Travel

1. Open **FCTVacations.pptx** and then save it with the name **2-FCTVacations**.
2. Display the Format Background task pane and make sure the fill options display. Apply the Radial Gradient - Accent 1 gradient fill color (first column, fifth row) and then apply the gradient fill to all slides in the presentation. *Hint: Use the Preset gradients button with the* **Gradient fill** *option selected in the* **Format Background task pane.**
3. Increase the font size of the subtitle *Vacation Specials* in Slide 1. (You determine the size.)
4. Apply bold formatting, the Gold, Accent 5, Lighter 80% font color (ninth column, second row in *Theme Colors* section), and left alignment to each heading in Slides 2 through 6.
5. Make Slide 1 active and then insert the **FCTLogo.jpg** file into the slide. Make the background of the logo transparent. You determine the size and position of the logo.
6. Apply any formatting you feel is necessary to improve the appearance of each slide.
7. Apply a transition and sound to each slide in the presentation.
8. Run the slide show.
9. Print the presentation as handouts with all six slides displayed horizontally on one page.
10. Save **2-FCTVacations.pptx**.

Assessment 3 Using the Tell Me Feature to Convert Text to a SmartArt Graphic

1. With **2-FCTVacations.pptx** open, make Slide 4 active and select all of the bulleted text.
2. Use the Tell Me feature to convert the bulleted text to a SmartArt graphic of your choosing.
3. Apply formatting to enhance the appearance of the SmartArt graphic.
4. Print only Slide 4.
5. Save and then close **2-FCTVacations.pptx**.

Assessment 4   Locating Information and Preparing a Presentation

1. Search for information on the Internet on your favorite author, historical figure, or entertainer.
2. Using PowerPoint, create a presentation with a minimum of four slides on the person you chose. Include a title slide with the person's name and your name and additional slides with information such as personal statistics, achievements, and awards.
3. Take an appropriate screenshot image of the person or something related to the person and insert it into any slide where it seems appropriate.
4. Apply a transition and sound to each slide in the presentation.
5. Save the presentation and name it **2-PerPres**.
6. Run the slide show.
7. Print the slides as handouts with six slides displayed horizontally per page.
8. Save and then close **2-PerPres.pptx**.

Marquee Challenge

Challenge 1   Preparing a Presentation for Worldwide Enterprises

1. Create the presentation shown in Figure WB-2.7. Apply the Retrospect design theme and the Blue II theme colors. Insert **WELogo.jpg** in Slide 1. In Slide 2, apply the Blue, Accent 2 font color (sixth column, first row in the *Theme Colors* section) to the title text and the Dark Blue font color (ninth option in the *Standard Colors* section) to the subtitle text. Insert the **Stockmarket.png** image in Slide 3. Change the color of the image to Blue, Accent color 2 Light (third column, third row in the *Recolor* section). Size and position the image as shown in the figure. Insert the **Package.png** image in Slide 6. Change the brightness and contrast to Brightness: +20% Contrast: -20% (fourth column, second row in the *Brightness/Contrast* section). Size and position the images as shown in the figure. Create and format the SmartArt graphic shown in Slide 5.
2. Save the completed presentation and name it **2-WEDist**.
3. Print the presentation as a handout with all six slides displayed horizontally on one page and then close the presentation.

Challenge 2   Preparing a Presentation for The Waterfront Bistro

1. Create the presentation shown in Figure WB-2.8. Apply the Dividend theme and the blue variant (second option in the Variants group). Change the slide size to Standard (4:3) and ensure fit. Insert **TWBLogo.jpg** in Slides 1 and 2 and then apply the Drop Shadow Rectangle picture style to the logo on both slides. Create and format the SmartArt organizational chart in Slide 3 using the Hierarchy SmartArt graphic. Create and format the SmartArt graphic shown in Slide 4. Insert the **Catering.png** image in Slide 6 and format and size the image as shown in the figure.
2. Save the completed presentation and name it **2-TWBInfo**.
3. Print the presentation as a handout with all six slides displayed horizontally on one page and then close the presentation.

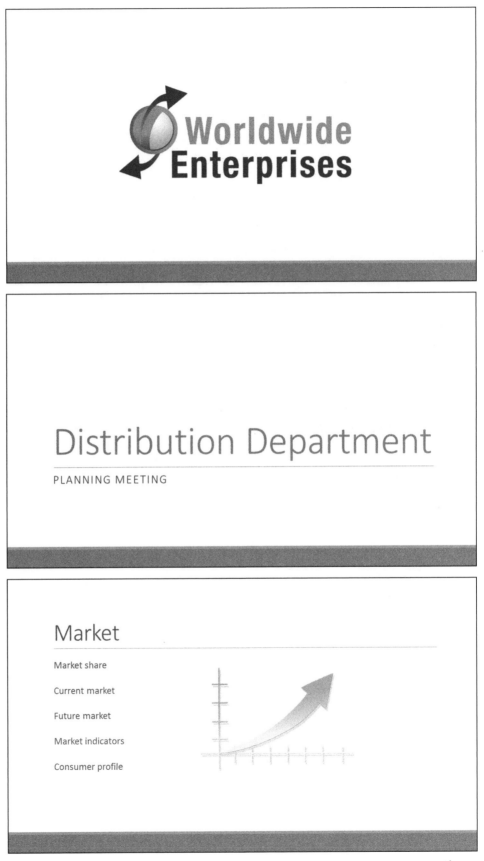

continues

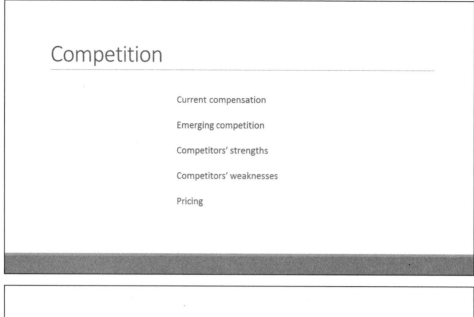

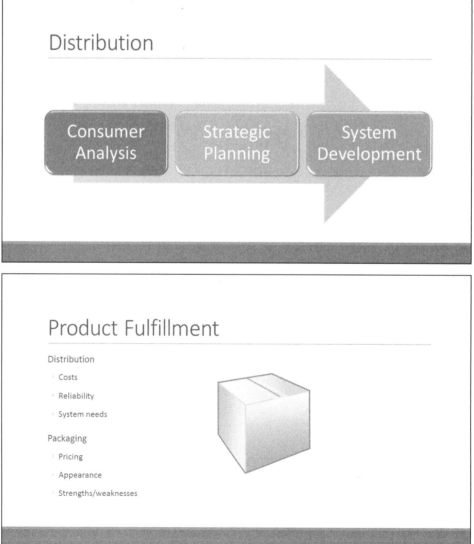

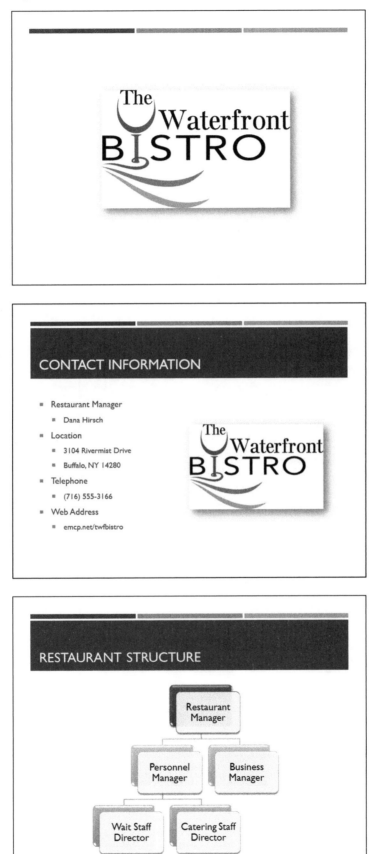

continues

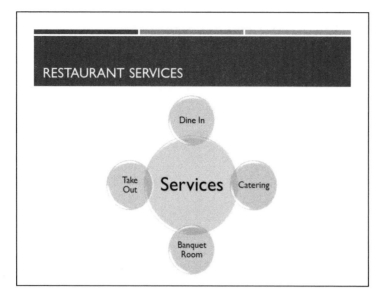

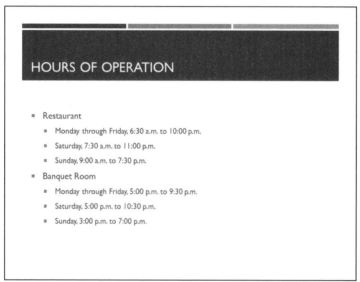

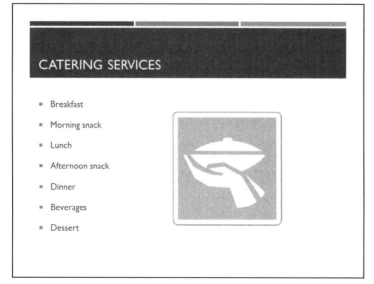

Study Tools

Study tools include a presentation and In Brief step lists. Use these resources to help you further develop and review skills learned in this section.

Knowledge Check

SNAP Check your understanding by identifying application tools used in this section. If you are a SNAP user, launch the Knowledge Check from your Assignments page.

Recheck

SNAP Check your understanding by taking this quiz. If you are a SNAP user, launch the Recheck from your Assignments page.

Skills Exercise

SNAP Additional activities are available to SNAP users. If you are a SNAP user, access these activities from your Assignments page.

Skills Review

Data Files

Review 1   Formatting and Customizing a Biography Project Presentation

1. Open **MPBiography.pptx** and then save it with the name **3-MPBiography**.
2. Make Slide 4 active, turn on the display of the Clipboard task pane, and then clear any contents in the task pane.
3. Select and then copy *Chris Greenbaum*.
4. Select and then copy *Camille Matsui*.
5. Select and then copy *Amy Eisman*.
6. Select and then copy *Tricia Becktold*.
7. Make Slide 5 active.
8. Position the insertion point immediately right of *On-Site Expenses*, press the Enter key, press the Tab key, and then click *Camille Matsui* in the Clipboard task pane.
9. Position the insertion point immediately right of *Benefits*, press the Enter key, press the Tab key, and then click *Chris Greenbaum* in the Clipboard task pane.
10. Position the insertion point immediately right of *Production*, press the Enter key, press the Tab key, and then click *Amy Eisman* in the Clipboard task pane.
11. Press the Enter key and then click *Tricia Becktold* in the Clipboard task pane.
12. Clear the contents of the Clipboard task pane and then close the task pane.

13. Make Slide 1 active and then find all occurrences of *Camille Matsui* and replace them with *Jennie Almonzo*.
14. Find all occurrences of *Tricia Becktold* and replace them with *Nick Jaffe*.
15. Make sure Slide 1 is active and then insert **MPLogo.jpg**. Size and position the logo on the slide.
16. Make Slide 2 active and then insert the name of the biography, *Silent Streets*, as WordArt. You determine the formatting and shape of the WordArt. Increase the size of the WordArt so it fills most of the slide and then horizontally and vertically center the WordArt in the slide.
17. Make Slide 6 active and then create the table shown in Figure WB-3.1. Apply the Medium Style 1 - Accent 1 table style (second column, first row in the *Medium* section), select all cells in the table, and then change the font size to 24 points. Size and position the table and table columns as shown. (Drag the column borders to decrease the size of the columns.)
18. Make Slide 7 active, create the arrows shown in Figure WB-3.2, and insert the text in the shapes as shown. Apply the Intense Effect - Lavender, Accent 1 shape style to the shapes (second column, sixth row in the *Theme Styles* section), apply the Lavender, Accent 2, Darker 50% shape outline (sixth column, last row in *Theme Colors* section), and then change the font size to 40 points. (If necessary, increase the size of the arrows to accommodate the larger font size.)
19. Make Slide 1 active and then draw an action button using the *Action Button: Forward or Next* option in the lower right corner of the slide. Fill the button with a color that complements the slide design. Copy the button and then paste it in Slides 2, 3, 4, 5, and 6.
20. Insert a footer that prints *Silent Streets* at the bottom of each slide.
21. Make Slide 4 active and then insert the **Team.png** image. You determine the size, positioning, and coloring of the image.
22. Make Slide 5 active and then insert the **Money.png** image. You determine the size, positioning, and coloring of the image.
23. Run the slide show beginning with Slide 1.
24. Print the presentation as handouts with four slides displayed horizontally per page. (The presentation will print on two pages.)
25. Save and then close **3-MPBiography.pptx**.

Figure WB-3.1 Slide 6

Activity	Date
Completed Script	October 30
Final Budget	November 8
Location Confirmation	November 8
Casting Decisions	January 1
Begin Filming	January 7

Figure WB-3.2 Slide 7

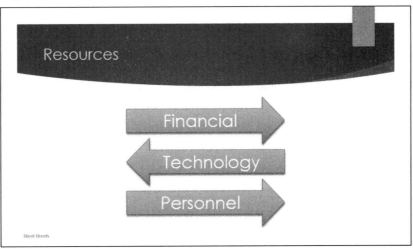

Review 2   Formatting with Slide Masters

1. Open **MPAnnualMtg.pptx** and then save it with the name **3-MPAnnualMtg**.
2. Apply the Facet design theme.
3. Display the presentation in Slide Master view, click the third slide thumbnail in the slide thumbnails pane (Title and Content Layout), and then make the following changes:
   - Apply the Aspect theme colors.
   - Change the theme fonts to Cambria.
   - Select the *Click to edit Master title style* placeholder text and then change the font color to Red, Accent 2 (sixth column, first row in the *Theme Colors* section) and the font size to 40 points.
   - Select the *Edit Master text styles* placeholder text and then change the font size to 24 points.
   - Select the *Second level* placeholder text and then change the font size to 20 points.
   - Insert the **MPLogo.jpg** file in the slide. Decrease the size of the logo so the height is approximately 0.5 inch. Drag the logo to the lower right corner of the master slide.
4. Close Slide Master view.
5. Apply a slide transition and transition sound to each slide.
6. Run the slide show.
7. Print the presentation as handouts with nine slides displayed horizontally per page.
8. Save and then close **3-MPAnnualMtg.pptx**.

Review 3   Formatting a Vacation Cruise Slide Show to Run Automatically

1. Open **FCTCruise.pptx** and then save the presentation with the name **3-FCTCruise**.
2. Make Slide 1 active and then insert the **FCTLogo.jpg** file. Size and position the logo on the slide.
3. Rehearse the timings and set the following times for the slides:

   Slide 1: 4 seconds   Slide 4: 4 seconds
   Slide 2: 8 seconds   Slide 5: 7 seconds
   Slide 3: 8 seconds

4. With Slide 1 active, insert **FCTAudioClip-03.mid**. With the Audio Tools Playback tab selected, change the *Start* option to *Automatically* and insert check marks in the *Play Across Slides* check box, the *Loop until Stopped* check box, and the *Hide During Show* check box.
5. Set up the slide show to run continuously.
6. Run the slide show and view it at least twice.
7. Print the presentation as handouts with six slides displayed horizontally per page.
8. Save and then close **3-FCTCruise.pptx**.

Skills Assessment

Assessment 1 Formatting a Presentation for Performance Threads

1. Open **PTCostumes.pptx** and then save it with the name **3-PTCostumes**.
2. With Slide 1 the active slide, insert **PTLogo.jpg**. Recolor the background to transparent color and size and position the company logo on the slide.
3. Make Slide 3 active and then insert the movie name *Ring of Roses* as WordArt. You determine the formatting, shape, size, and position of the WordArt in the slide.
4. Make Slide 5 the active slide, create a shape (you determine the shape), and then copy the shape two times (so the slide contains a total of three shapes). Insert *Research* in the first shape, *Design* in the second shape, and *Production* in the third shape. Format, size, and position the shapes in the slide.
5. Make Slide 6 the active slide and then insert the following information in a table (apply a table style and increase the size of the table to better fill the slide):

Designer	Date
Scott Bercini	June 21
Terri Cantrell	June 13
Paul Gottlieb	June 28
Tae Jeong	June 13
Rosa Levens	June 28

6. Insert the footer *Performance Threads* at the bottom of each slide.
7. Run the slide show.
8. Print the presentation as handouts with four slides displayed horizontally per page (the presentation will print on two pages).
9. Save and then close **3-PTCostumes.pptx**.

Assessment 2 Formatting a Presentation for First Choice Travel

1. Open **FCTSouthernTours.pptx** and then save the presentation with the name **3-FCTSouthernTours**.
2. Make Slide 2 active and then insert *Australia* as WordArt. You determine the formatting, size, and position of the WordArt in the slide.
3. Make Slide 6 active and then insert *New Zealand* as WordArt. You determine the formatting, size, and position of the WordArt in the slide.
4. Insert a footer that prints *SOUTHERN TOURS* at the bottom of each slide.
5. Rehearse the timings and determine the seconds for each slide.
6. Insert the audio file **FCTAudioClip-04.mid** that will automatically play across all slides and loop until stopped.
7. Set up the slide show to run continuously.

8. Run the slide show and view it at least twice.
9. Print the presentation as handouts with nine slides displayed horizontally per page.
10. Save and then close **3-FCTSouthernTours.pptx**.

Assessment 3   Learning about Custom Slide Shows

1. Open **3-FCTSouthernTours.pptx** and then save it with the name **3-FCTSouthernToursCustom**.
2. Use the Help feature and/or experiment with the Custom Slide Show button in the Start Slide Show group on the Slide Show tab to learn about custom slide shows.
3. Create a custom slide show containing Slides 1, 7, 8, and 9. (You determine the name of the show.)
4. Run the custom slide show.
5. Save and then close **3-FCTSouthernToursCustom.pptx**.

INDIVIDUAL CHALLENGE

Assessment 4   Locating Information and Preparing a Presentation on Social Networking Sites

1. Using the Internet, search for social networking sites. Identify five sites that interest you (or that you currently use).
2. Using PowerPoint, create a presentation about the sites (one site per slide) that includes information about the sites and hyperlinks to each site. Create a title slide for the presentation that includes your name and an appropriate title. (You should have a total of six slides.) To add visual appeal to your presentation, insert at least two elements, such as WordArt, shapes, and/or images.
3. Apply animation to objects in the slides.
4. Save the presentation and name it **3-SocialNetwork**.
5. Run the slide show.
6. Print the presentation as handouts with six slides displayed horizontally per page.
7. Save and then close **3-SocialNetwork.pptx**.

Marquee Challenge

Challenge 1   Preparing a Project Schedule Presentation for Marquee Productions

1. Create the presentation shown in Figure WB-3.3 on the next two pages with the following specifications:
   - Apply the Retrospect design theme and the Yellow theme color.
   - Display the presentation in Slide Master view and then click the third slide thumbnail in the slide thumbnails pane. Change the font size of the master title style text to 44 points, apply bold formatting, and then change the font color to Orange, Accent 2. Change the font size of the first level master text style to 24 points. Close Slide Master view.
   - Delete the title placeholder in Slide 1 and then insert the **MPLogo.jpg** file. Size and position the logo as shown in the figure.
   - Center the subtitle text.
   - Insert the shape in Slide 2 using the Horizontal Scroll shape in the *Stars and Banners* section of the Shapes button drop-down list.
   - Create and format the table shown in Slide 3.

- Insert the **Finance.png** image in Slide 4 and then insert the **Team.png** image in Slide 5. Format, size, and position the images as shown in the figure.
- Insert the footer on all slides (except the first slide) as shown in the figure. *Hint: Insert a check mark in the* **Don't show on title slide** *check box in the Header and Footer dialog box.*

2. Save the completed presentation and name it **3-MPProdSch**.
3. Run the slide show.
4. Print the presentation as a handout with all six slides displayed horizontally per page.

Challenge 2   Preparing a Moroccan Tour Presentation for First Choice Travel

1. Create the presentation shown in Figure WB-3.4 on workbook pages WB-34 and WB-35 with these specifications:
   - Apply the Ion design theme and the Orange variant color.
   - Create the WordArt text in Slide 1.
   - Insert the **FCTLogo.jpg** file in the Slide Master view so it displays on Slides 3 through 6. Size and position the logo as shown in Figure WB-3.4.
   - Create the shape in Slide 2 using the Bevel shape in the *Basic Shapes* section of the Shapes button drop-down list.
   - Insert the **Desert.png** image in Slide 3 and the **City.png** image in Slide 5.
   - Create and format the table in Slide 6.

2. Save the completed presentation and name it **3-FCTMorocco**.
3. Run the slide show.
4. Print the presentation as a handout with six slides displayed horizontally per page.

Figure WB-3.3 Challenge 1

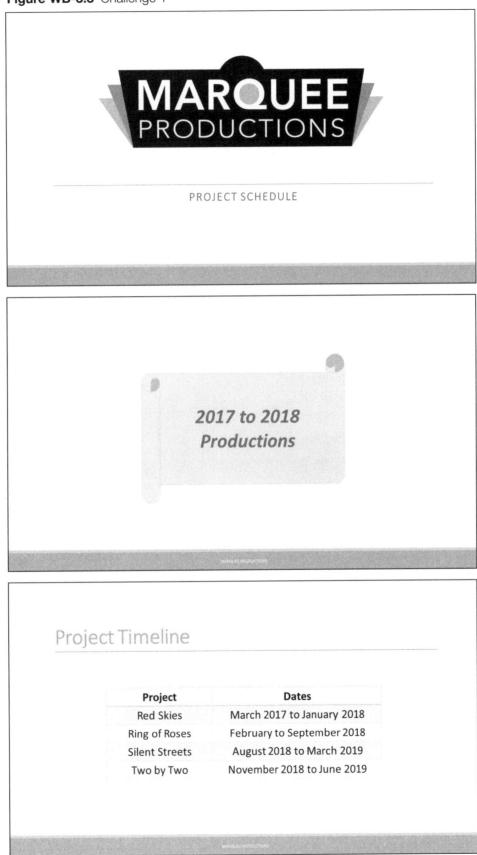

continues

Finances

On-site expenses

Location expenses

Production

Salaries

Benefits

Production Team

Production Manager

Finance Director

Script Director

Casting Director

Locations Director

Project Leaders

Red Skies, Amy Eisman

Ring of Roses, Chris Greenbaum

Silent Streets, Randall Seifert

Two by Two, Josh Hart

Figure WB-3.4 Challenge 2

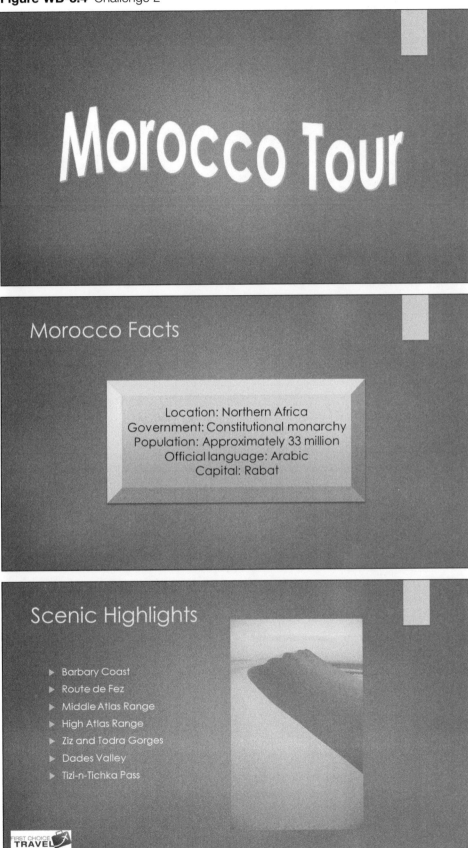

continues

Accommodations

- Casablanca: Royal Meridien
- Fez: Zalagh Plaza
- Erfoud: Le Berbere Resort
- Ouarzazate: Belere Palace
- Marrakesh: Saadi Hotel

Itinerary

- Casablanca: Three days, two nights
- Fez: Three days, two nights
- Erfoud: Two days, one night
- Marrakesh: Two days, one night

Dates and Prices

Dates	Land and Air	Land Only
January 17 through 27	$2,359	$1,599
March 8 through 18	$2,359	$1,599
June 6 through 16	$2,119	$1,399
September 20 through 30	$2,119	$1,399

Study Tools

Study tools include a presentation and In Brief step lists. Use these resources to help you further develop and review skills learned in this section.

Recheck

SNAP Check your understanding by taking this quiz. If you are a SNAP user, launch the Recheck from your Assignments page.

Skills Review

Review 1   Exporting a PowerPoint Presentation to Word

Data File

1. Open Word and PowerPoint.
2. With PowerPoint active, open **FCTVacations.pptx** and then save it with the name **3-FCTVacations**.
3. Send the PowerPoint data to Word. Click the *Blank lines next to slides* option and the *Paste link* option at the Send to Microsoft Word dialog box.
4. Save the Word document and name it **3-FCTVacSpecials**.
5. Print and then close **3-FCTVacSpecials.docx**.
6. Click the PowerPoint button on the taskbar.
7. Make Slide 4 active and then change *$1,150* to *$1,250*, *$1,275* to *$1,375*, and *$1,315* to *$1,415*.
8. Save the presentation and then print Slide 4.
9. Make Word active, open **3-FCTVacSpecials.docx**, and then click the Yes button at the message asking if you want to update the link.
10. Print only page 2 of **3-FCTVacSpecials.docx**.
11. Save and then close the document.
12. Make PowerPoint active and then close **3-FCTVacations.pptx**.

NIAGARA PENINSULA COLLEGE

Review 2   Linking and Editing an Excel Chart in a PowerPoint Slide

Data Files

1. Make sure PowerPoint is open and then open Excel.
2. Make PowerPoint active and then open **NPCEnroll.pptx**.
3. Save the presentation with the name **3-NPCEnroll**.
4. Make Slide 4 active.
5. Make Excel active and then open **NPCEnrollChart.xlsx**. Save the workbook with the name **3-NPCEnrollChart**.

6. Click the chart to select it (make sure you select the entire chart and not just a chart element) and then copy and link the chart to Slide 4 in **3-NPCEnroll.pptx**. (Be sure to use the Paste Special dialog box.)
7. Increase the size of the chart to better fill the slide and then center it on the slide.
8. Click outside the chart to deselect it.
9. Save the presentation, print only Slide 4, and then close the presentation.
10. Click the Excel button on the taskbar.
11. Click outside the chart to deselect it.
12. Insert another department in the worksheet (and chart) by making cell A7 active, clicking the Insert button arrow in the Cells group on the Home tab, and then clicking *Insert Sheet Rows* at the drop-down list. (This creates a new row 7.) Type the following text in the specified cells:
    - A7: Directing
    - B7: 18
    - C7: 32
    - D7: 25
13. Click in cell A4.
14. Save, print, and close **3-NPCEnrollChart.xlsx** and then close Excel.
15. Click the PowerPoint button on the taskbar and then open **3-NPCEnroll.pptx**. At the message telling you that the presentation contains links, click the Update Links button.
16. Display Slide 4 and note the change to the chart.
17. Save the presentation, print only Slide 4, and then close the presentation.

NIAGARA PENINSULA COLLEGE

Data File

Review 3 Embedding and Editing a Word Table in a PowerPoint Slide

1. With Word and PowerPoint open, make PowerPoint active and then open **3-NPCEnroll.pptx**. At the message telling you that the presentation contains links, click the Update Links button.
2. Make Slide 5 active.
3. Make Word active and then open **NPCContacts.docx**.
4. Select the table and then copy and embed it in Slide 5 in **3-NPCEnroll.pptx**. (Make sure you use the Paste Special dialog box.)
5. With the table selected in the slide, use the sizing handles to increase the size and change the position of the table so it better fills the slide.
6. Click outside the table to deselect it and then save the presentation.
7. Double-click the table, select *Editing* in the name *Emerson Editing*, and then type Edits.
8. Click outside the table to deselect it.
9. Print Slide 5 of the presentation.
10. Apply a transition and transition sound of your choosing to all slides in the presentation.
11. Run the slide show.
12. Save and then close **3-NPCEnroll.pptx** and then close PowerPoint.
13. Close **NPCContacts.docx** and then close Word.